GAMES ON
THRONES

An Hachette UK Company
www.hachette.co.uk

First published in Great Britain in 2015 by Hamlyn, a
division of Octopus Publishing Group Ltd, Carmelite
House, 50 Victoria Embankment, London, EC4Y 0DZ
www.octopusbooksusa.com

This edition published in 2018.

Distributed in the US by Hachette Book Group
1290 Avenue of the Americas, 4th and 5th Floors, New
York, NY 10104

Distributed in Canada by Canadian Manda Group
664 Annette St., Toronto, Ontario, Canada M6S 2C8

Text by Michael Powell
Design by Milestone Creative
Bespoke photography © Jonathan Pollock 2015, 2018
Ink drawings by Jon Davies

ISBN 978-0-600-63533-8

Printed and bound in China
10 9 8 7 6 5 4 3 2 1

INTRODUCTION

Here you sit on the Porcelain Throne, besieged in your
tiny tiled kingdom. It is a most challenging realm,
where pain softens into pleasure and winter becomes
summer, where dangerous undercurrents, restless
movements and violent alimentary struggles battle for
your attention. Several times a day, you must obey its
aquatic subpoenas to bend the knee, answer the call
and perform your dark business.

Despite all this visceral drama, sitting on the loo
remains one of the most boring things you can do.
So it's smart to BYOD (Bring Your Own Distraction)
while you wait for the barbarians to rattle the gate.

Help is at hand. Or rather, in your hand.
This bonanza of games, tricks, puzzles and projects
will provide hours of fun for all the family, challenge
your mental abilities and creativity and keep you
entertained through even the longest bathroom break.
There's something for everyone to enjoy,
so don't pay a visit without it.

ORIGAMI DRAGON

Dragons are massive, flying reptiles which breathe fire onto their enemies, lay waste to armies and burn entire cities to the ground.
Create your own flapping serpentine sentinel to shore up your power base and survey your porcelain empire.

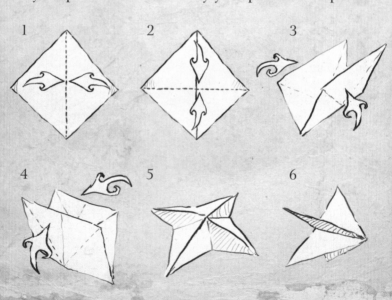

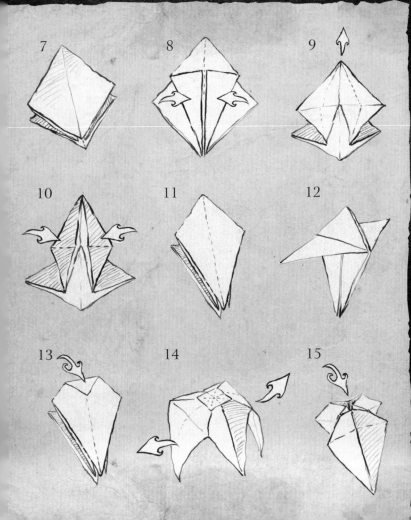

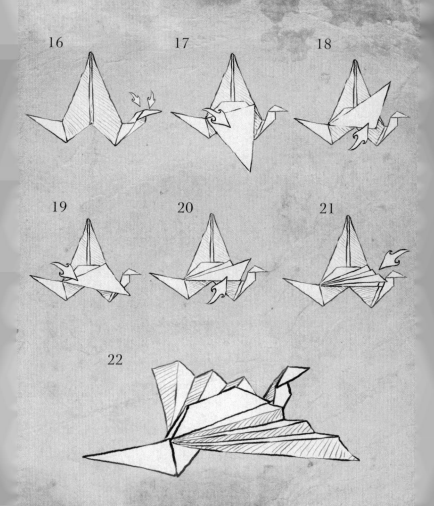

16   17   18

19   20   21

22

PRINCE OR PRINCESS?

A king has two children. One of them is a boy. What is the probability that the other is a girl?

Hint: the correct answer is NOT fifty per cent.

POISONED PIES

Three pies are brought to the royal banquet table of a greedy king. His spies have informed him that two of the pies have been poisoned but they are such delicious pies that he doesn't want to throw all three away. So he gives the first pie to his taster Rosencrantz, the second pie to his other taster Guildenstern and keeps the third. Rosencrantz takes a bite out of the first pie and collapses on the floor, writhing in agony. So now the king knows that one of the other two pies is safe to eat, but he doesn't want to share any of the good pie, so he snatches Guildenstern's and starts eating it, reasoning that this pie now gives him the lowest chance of being poisoned. Was the king's reasoning correct?

COAT OF ARMS

Which coat of arms comes next in the sequence?

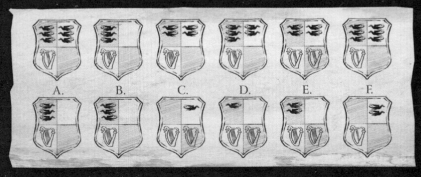

BATHROOM TILES

Stare at the tiles on your bathroom floor imagining that they are flagstones beneath the throne at court. How many different rectangles can you make out of these eight tiles?

MATCHSTICKS
& TOILET ROLL

How can you arrange ten matchsticks so they form a circle with the same diameter as a toilet roll tube, while ensuring that each match is no closer than one centimetre away from any other match?

THREE PRIVIES

The King has three royal privies in his castle, one in the West Turret, one in the East Turret and the third in the South Turret. Each privy is lit by a single light bulb, but all three switches are located in the King's bedroom in the North Turret. The impatient king summons his Groom of the Stool and demands to know which switch operates which bulb. The Groom is recovering from a nasty bout of food poisoning, so he earnestly desires to perform his duty with the minimum of travelling. What should he do?

MAKE A MUSKET
FROM A BALLOON & A TOILET ROLL TUBE

YOU WILL NEED:

A round balloon (not a sausage), toilet roll tube, pair of scissors, tape.

1. Cut the neck off the balloon just below the point where it meets the body.

2. Stretch the mouth of the balloon over one end of the toilet roll tube and secure with tape.

3. Select your ammunition and drop it into the open end of the barrel.

Now that you're locked in and loaded, set up a row of toilet roll tubes along the rim of the bath, take aim with your musket and spend half an hour re-enacting your favourite Kevin Costner film. Just you, your musket and a bag of coins.

Enjoy the drama as dozens of tiny copper-plated steel discs ricochet off the walls, crack tiles, smash your bathroom mirror and, if you're really persistent, detach your retinas. Alternatively, if you value your bathroom fixtures and your eyesight, experiment with safer ammunition such as cotton wool buds, cut-up pieces of sponge or wads of wet toilet paper.

THREE
MORAL CONUNDRUMS

Did you know that women spend on average about one hour 25 minutes a week on the toilet? Men spend even longer – about one hour 45 minutes. That's between 2 and 2.5 working weeks a year, depending on your gender, which is a considerable chunk of time available for self-improvement.

So, why not exercise your grey matter and ponder these three moral conundrums to confound your brain tank? In keeping with Kant's view that morality is based on human reason rather than utility or natural laws, there are no right or wrong answers here, so knock yourself out.

1. DUNGEON DILEMMA

The tyrant king has incarcerated you, your son and twelve other innocent people in the castle dungeon for life. Your son tries to escape but he is caught by the guards and sentenced to death. You face a choice: either your son is hanged, or you can spare his life by choosing another prisoner to take his place. You must kick away the chair.

2. KNIGHTMARE

A ruthless knight takes two children hostage and intends to behead them and then fall on his sword unless you (the King) agree to his single demand: bring his sister to him so that he can kill her instead. She is a good person and an excellent mother with three dependent children. However, it is common knowledge that they are incestuous lovers. If you deny his demand, the two children will die. There is no possibility of negotiation or rescue. What do you do?

3. PEACE OFFERING

A terminally ill king has a few hours to live. He has two daughters, one good and one evil. If the king dies before sunset the good daughter will become queen; if he dies after sunset the evil daughter will become queen, execute her sister and declare war on the neighbouring kingdom. Is the good daughter justified in killing her father before sunset to save her life and maintain peace?

DESERT ISLAND

Here is a list of thirty objects. Pick five at random and think about the most creative ways you can use them to help you to escape from a desert island.

Lamp	Button	Marble
Tomatoes	Lettuce	Wheel
Bomb	Cherries	Butter
Scarf	Doll	Ants
Kittens	Coat	Soap
Fruit	Cream	Crown
Stove	Cobweb	Quartz
Pump	Pizza	Sofa
Bath	Hat	Gun
Coal	Celery	Cheese

TOILET HAIKU

A haiku is a Japanese poem with three lines consisting of five, seven and five syllables respectively. Pick three words at random from the list above and write a haiku using one of the words on each line.

For example, choosing 'cheese', 'soap' and 'pizza' you might say:

Without melted cheese
Soap will taste quite unpleasant
Pizza is better

THE LOYALTY QUIZ

Kingdoms, families and relationships all depend on loyalty to function effectively. Loyalty binds us together but it also divides us, drives nations into fruitless wars and allows unspeakable acts of evil to be committed in its name.

So how loyal are you? Does it trump your morality and suspend your reason or are you capable of seeing the wider picture and the greater good?

1. YOU LOVE YOUR JOB AND WORK IN A TEAM WITH THREE OTHER PEOPLE WHOM YOU CONSIDER TO BE GOOD FRIENDS AS WELL AS COLLEAGUES. ONE MORNING YOUR BOSS TELLS YOU THERE'S A FIFTY PER CENT CHANCE SHE WILL HAVE TO LIQUIDATE THE COMPANY IN THE NEAR FUTURE. YOU'VE BEEN OFFERED ANOTHER JOB WITH THE SAME SALARY AND JOB SECURITY. IF YOU LEAVE, THE COMPANY WILL IMMEDIATELY FOLD AND YOUR THREE FRIENDS WILL BE UNEMPLOYED. WHAT DO YOU DO?

a. Stay put, stick with your friends and tell no one about the job offer.

b. Discuss the decision with your colleagues to get their opinion.

c. Accept the new job. I feel bad, but if they're true friends, they'll understand.

d. Accept the new job – they'd do the same to me.

2. WHAT HAS TO HAPPEN BEFORE YOU'RE PREPARED TO TRUST A NEW FRIEND?

a. Nothing. I just follow my instinct about them.

b. I can't expect to earn their trust unless I trust them back.

c. I wait for tangible proof that they are trustworthy.

d. You can't trust many people, so I'll probably always keep my guard up.

3. WHICH MOST ACCURATELY DESCRIBES YOUR RELATIONSHIP WITH OLD FRIENDS?

a. I trust them implicitly, otherwise they wouldn't be my friends.

b. They can trust me with their secrets and vice versa.

c. I'd be honest with them if they needed to hear an uncomfortable truth.

d. I'd do anything for them, but if they broke my trust I would cut them off forever.

4. WHAT DO YOU VALUE MOST IN A FRIENDSHIP?

a. I like to feel needed.

b. Being told what I need to hear.

c. Being able to be myself.

d. Loyalty.

5. YOUR BEST FRIEND'S EX-PARTNER DECLARES THEIR LOVE FOR YOU AND YOU FEEL THE SAME WAY. WHAT DO YOU DO?

a. Do nothing, in loyalty to your friend.

b. Talk to your friend and abide by his/her wishes.

c. Talk to your friend to explain why you are going to follow your heart.

d. Love trumps friendship, deal with it.

THE LOYALTY QUIZ: RESULTS

MOSTLY A

Your loyalty knows no bounds. You are open, instinctive, unselfish and always consider the needs and feelings of others above your own. However, your trusting nature leaves you vulnerable to exploitation. You may well feel that's a necessary risk but if you suffer from low self esteem, it can only improve when you begin to pay more attention to your own happiness.

MOSTLY B

You are a caring and loyal friend, with a strong sense of your own separate identity. You believe in effective communication and recognize that friendship is a reciprocal process where trust is given and earned. You strive to do the right thing and be authentic, but you should also acknowledge that sometimes life just gets messy and can't always be micromanaged.

MOSTLY C

You take a very pragmatic approach to your relationships and you expect others to take you on your own terms. You like to appear strong and you're not afraid to jeopardize a friendship to pursue your own agenda, but you may regret this approach in later life when all your chips have been cashed in and the cost–benefit analysis is complete.

MOSTLY D

You have some serious trust issues, my friend. It's all or nothing with you. You honour the code of omertà but heaven help anyone who breaks your trust because they won't get a second chance. For you, life is a zero sum game and you intend to come out on top every time. No matter who gets hurt, you'll do anything to ensure it's not you.

THREE SLAVES BET

The King of the North made the Queen of the South an offer she couldn't refuse. 'I bet you one slave, that if you give me two slaves I promise I will give you three slaves in return. Do you accept my offer?'

Should the Queen of the South accept the bet?

BURNING ISLAND

A vindictive king has devised a cruel method to execute five of his enemy prisoners. He calls it 'Death by Burning Island'.

The five prisoners are airlifted to the east side of a small island that is covered in thick forest and surrounded by high cliffs. Anyone trying to escape by jumping into the sea will be dashed on the rocks or killed upon impact with the water.

The wind is blowing from west to east. The king's henchmen set light to the forest on the west side of the island and then fly away. There is no escape for the five prisoners, who must wait for the fire to spread towards them and burn them alive.

They have no way of putting out the fire. No ropes, to climb down the cliffs, no means of protection. Just a single unused match in its box. How can they survive the inferno?

GUINEVERE'S GRANDMOTHER

Guinevere's grandmother is two years older than her mother. How is this possible?

DOODLE
YOUR OWN CISTERN SIGIL

A sigil is a magic symbol that helps you manifest your heart's desires. The bathroom is a place of wonder, where the improbable can become the possible because it's one of the few places in our busy day where we can ruminate alone.
If you stay present and manifest positive energy while you are on the throne, your subconscious will work to produce healthy outcomes in your life; but if you focus on negative thoughts and feelings, you will probably leave the bathroom with your flies undone or the hem of your skirt tucked into your knickers.

Sitting on the toilet is the perfect time to calm your mind and create a sigil, especially since the materials you need are close at hand. All you need is a toilet roll rube, a marker pen and a pair of scissors.

1. Cut the toilet roll tube along its entire length and open it out to form a rectangle.

2. Breathe slowly in through your nose and out through your mouth as you think of a statement of intent. Something you want to happen or to make happen. As you continue to relax into the breathing, condense your statement into a short sentence. For example, it might be 'I WANT TO WIN THE LOTTERY'.

3. Now take each letter of the sentence and draw them in order on the rectangle with confident strokes of the marker pen, omitting any repeats. The sentence above would

WANTOHELRY and
might end up looking
g like the above.

ch the sigil to the
d let it work its magic.
v on, every time you
bathroom you will see
erious symbol,
your subconscious to
your wish. Also

to the toilet, they
hard about what
which also sends
energy into the c
The more people
to unravel its mys
stronger its magic
This is why a pub
convenience is th
place to leave you
turn your dreams

SEVEN ARROWS

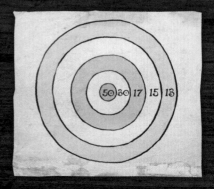

1. Using exactly seven arrows, how can an archer score 103?

2. What is the minimum number of arrows required to reach 103?

HOW LONG IS THIS
JOUSTING TILT?

Complete this sentence so that it accurately describes the length of each individual jousting tilt while being simultaneously true in all three cases.

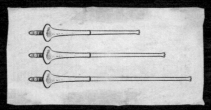

The length of this tilt is _____.

HOW MANY DROPS OF WINE?

How many drops of wine can be put in an empty flagon?

MAKE YOUR OWN
BATHROOM SKITTLES

If you've been living on omelettes all week or you've neglected your dietary fibre regime and know that you're in for a long bathroom session, bar skittles can be a great way to pass the time and is preferable to getting an embolism by rushing the job. This game is based on the traditional pub skittles game 'Devil Amongst the Tailors' but it's been specially adapted for the bathroom environment.

YOU WILL NEED:
Dental floss in a dispenser, sticky tape and nine toilet roll tubes.

SETTING UP THE GAME

1. Attach the end of the dental floss to the ceiling, about one metre (3 feet) in front of the toilet. You can tie it to the light fitting, or use a drawing pin.

2. Unwind the floss so that it almost touches the floor, then secure with sticky tape so no more floss can unravel from the dispenser. The dispenser should be able to swing freely at the bottom of the length of floss. Depending on the layout of your bathroom, you may face obstructions that make game play more challenging. This is to be expected and gives your home ground its unique characteristics.

3. Sit on the toilet and stand nine toilet roll tubes in a diamond shape on the floor in front of you.

PLAYING THE GAME

1. You have three swings.

2. Swing the dental floss in an arc away from you and catch when it returns. On its journey, it must knock down the front skittle furthest away from you to score. Score one point for each fallen skittle and remove. If the front skittle is still standing, you must stand all the fallen skittles back up.

3. You can score a maximum of 27 points by knocking down all nine skittles on each of your three throws.

PIMP
MY THRONE

'SO YOU WANNA BE A PLAYER, BUT YOUR PRIVY AIN'T DAPPER? YOU GOTTA HIT IT UP, TO GET A PIMPED-OUT CRAPPER.'

The only thing standing between you and a pimped out WC is your wallet and the size of your dreams. If you can dream big you can build crazy.

Here are five crunk ideas that take khazi customizing to a completely different level. Transform your lacklustre thinking chair into an impressive new ride.

1. PUMP UP THE VOLUME

When the float valve in the toilet cistern needs to be replaced, it will make a foghorn noise when flushed! So get the lid off and replace the washer with a piece of worn-out rubber.

2. BRING THE BLING

Replace any metal fixings with gold plate. It's not even expensive. Why settle for chrome when you can grab yourself a ceramic and gold-plated toilet cistern lever flush handle on eBay for less than twenty big ones?

3. GET BUSY WITH THE SLOGANS

Nothing is classier than a pithy slogan on your toilet lid. You can use a stencilling kit or just get creative with a marker pen, but whatever you do, don't leave it blank. You can pick up tasteful vinyl wall decals for next to nothing, including these three classics:

> ## 'GO HITHER!'
> ## 'DO AS THOU WILT.'
> ## 'PRITHEE, DO NOT THROW YOUR BUSINESS OUT OF THE WINDOW. USE THE FLUSH HANDLE.'

4. UNDER-RIM LIGHTING

Attach a string of battery-operated neon LEDs underneath the rim for crisp, clear bright light – with built-in noise activation that will turn on every time it detects a sound. No more stumbling around in the dark or urinating up the wall in the middle of the night.

5. PUT A PLASMA TV IN IT

There's few things on earth that can't be improved with a plasma telly, or a drinks cabinet, fish tank, DJ turntables, subwoofers, popcorn popper, massage chair and mini pizza oven. Gadgets are irresistible, especially in the bathroom.

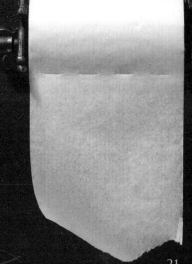

21

MAKE A BADASS
CROWN
FROM TOILET PAPER ROLLS

A fearless bathroom sovereign will always exude slick poise, but this impressive toilet paper roll crown will effortlessly increase the stature of even the most charismatic deuce dropper. The ingenious iterative construction method allows you to make a crown to accommodate any head size.

1. Simply cut open a toilet roll tube, lengthways, so you get two rectangles, approximately 7 cm by 10.5 cm (2.75 in x 4 in).

2. Photocopy the two templates, cut around the dotted line, staple them to your rectangles and then use scissors, a craft knife and a hole punch to cut out the silhouettes.

3. Staple the silhouettes together at the base.

4. Repeat steps 1 to 3 until the crown fits your head.

5. Spray gold or matt black.

6. For additional ceremonial bling, round off with acrylic jewels available from any good craft shop.

THE TYRANT QUIZ

Being a tyrant is harder than it looks. It requires dedication, a ridiculous haircut, a complete lack of self-knowledge, an external locus of control and the unshakeable belief that stability can be achieved through violence. If nothing else, tyrants are masters of cliché, whether in public life or their taste in interior decor. So do you have what it takes to be a ruthless and paranoid despot?

1. WHICH OF THESE OUTCOMES GIVES YOU THE GREATEST SATISFACTION?

a. Good people being rewarded.

b. Bad people being punished.

c. Bad things happening to good people.

d. Who cares? Anything could happen.

2. YOU HAVE BEEN SWEPT TO POWER IN A BLOODY COUP. WHAT'S YOUR FIRST ACTION AS THE NEW SUPREME LEADER?

a. Announce a national holiday.

b. Imprison all your political opponents.

c. Kill all your political opponents.

d. Kill all your political opponents and melt down their gold fillings to make taps for your bidet.

3. WHICH MOTTO BEST SUMS UP YOUR STYLE OF RULE?

a. Do unto others as you would have them do unto you.

b. Let's stay on the road to a stronger economy.

c. Dare to think, dare to act.

d. Let them hate, so long as they fear.

4. **YOU AND YOUR ROYAL CONSORT HAVE FAILED TO PRODUCE AN HEIR TO INHERIT YOUR DYNASTY. HOW DO YOU REACT?**

a. Appreciate that you had a good innings and that all things must come to an end.

b. File for divorce.

c. Found a new state religion to legitimize your divorce, then behead your next spouse.

d. Murder everyone with a legitimate claim to the throne and put their heads on spikes.

5. **YOUR REIGN FINALLY COMES TO ITS INEVITABLE CONCLUSION AS YOUR BRUTALIZED SUBJECTS SURROUND YOUR COMPOUND, BAYING FOR BLOOD. EVEN THE ARMY HAS DESERTED YOU. YOU HAVE FIVE MINUTES BEFORE THEY BREACH THE GATES. WHAT DO YOU DO?**

a. Die on your feet, weapon in hand.

b. Commit suicide in your bunker.

c. Commit suicide in your bunker, along with your partner and children.

d. Escape to Switzerland, Saudi Arabia, Paraguay or Morocco, take over the top two floors of the Novotel Hotel and live out the rest of your days in luxurious exile.

THE TYRANT QUIZ: RESULTS

MOSTLY A

You try to lead the good life and reward the loyalty and good behaviour of your subjects. You are probably a keen gardener and like nothing better than to potter about on your estate, tending the royal greenhouses or pretending to be a milkmaid. Benevolent and unskilled in the dark arts of realpolitik you may be, and at least you believe your actions benefit others, but you're still a freeloader who deserves to meet a sticky end.

MOSTLY B

You are capable of achieving a realistic tyranny–life balance, despite your unattractive sense of entitlement. You know what you want and how to get it, and you accept that collateral damage is an intrinsic part of pragmatic authoritarian leadership. However, you do have the tendency to be a little out of touch with ordinary folk and you haven't the first clue about the price of milk.

MOSTLY C

You don't even try to be a nice person. You probably lack intelligence so you mistrust intellectuals, modern technology and anyone called Nigel. Your paranoia and economic illiteracy will bring the country to its knees. Rather than feed your people, your tiny brain and relentless will to power mean you'll blow the nation's wealth on military infrastructure quicker than you can say 'agrarian collectivization'.

MOSTLY D

Your deranged and evil exploits make Heliogabalus look like George Monbiot. Your cruelty, profligacy and sexual perversity know no limits. Keeping up with the Kardashians is a walk in the park for you, since you clearly consider yourself a living god. For you, life is like a box of chocolates: rich, indulgent and absurdly expensive. The wheels of state fell off some time ago, so expect a bumpy ride during the short time you have left. History will not be kind.

THREE
MORAL CONUNDRUMS

If you thought the ethical dilemmas posed on page 10 were taxing, things are about to get much worse. Here are three more agonizing choices to generate cognitive dissonance. Remember to strike a match or open a window after you've wrestled with these knotty complications.

1. CAVE COLLAPSE

You and three other people are exploring a cave system deep underground when the roof collapses, crushing the legs of one of your team mates and trapping all of you in a tiny chamber. You calculate that carbon dioxide will reach saturation levels and kill you all within the next 24 hours. You know that a search party will be scrambled and you can expect to be rescued in 28 hours' time. If you fail to stem the bleeding of the injured team mate, she will die quickly, allowing you and the other two cavers to be rescued alive. Should you give her painkillers so she dies without pain, or do you stop the bleeding and keep her alive in the certainty that you will all die within 24 hours?

2. BLIND OR HALF-BLIND?

Would you rather half-blind a family member or completely blind a stranger?

3. RUNAWAY HORSE

A runaway horse is galloping towards a group of five children who are sitting on the grass. You are standing above them on a bridge. A morbidly obese stranger is also standing on the bridge. The only way you can save the children is to push the stranger off the bridge so that he lands on the rampaging animal, killing him and the horse. Should you commit murder to save five innocent lives?

TOILET ROLL TUBE
STATEMENT
JEWELLERY

If you like to loll around the house in your pyjamas, sweatpants or a onesie, this standout accessory will add the finishing touches to an otherwise lacklustre outfit. A toilet roll tube necklace is the perfect versatile ornament when you want to make a lasting impression.

1.

Photocopy the template opposite, then glue it to a toilet roll tube that has been cut open.

2.

Use scissors, a craft knife and a hole punch to carefully remove all the shaded areas and cut along every solid fan line.

3.

Score and then fold along the dotted lines.

4.

Spray paint both sides of the piece gold and/or silver and allow to dry.

5.

Thread a piece of toilet paper yarn (see page 48) through the holes and tie it around your neck.

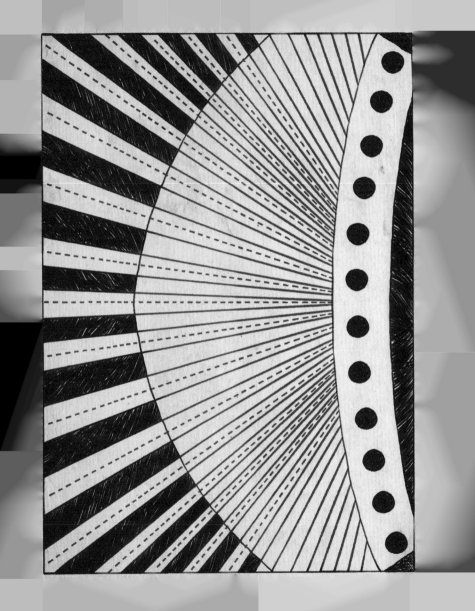

MAKE A HOUSE BANNER

Anyone who maintains a throne needs a bathroom banner that expresses their voiding style. Photocopy these two pages, cut out the square and circle and glue them to pieces of cardboard the same size.

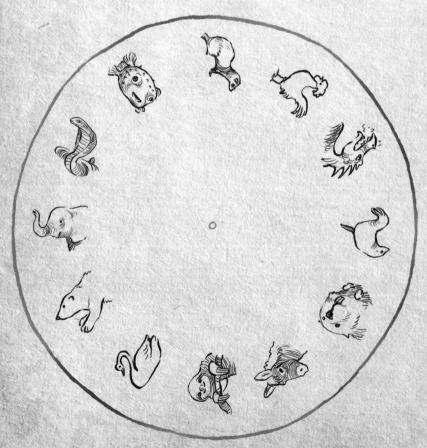

Use a craft knife to cut out a viewing window, then attach the disc
behind the banner with a clipper paper fastener. Each time you
perform a grunt sculpture, simply turn the disc to display the animal that
best represents its unique characteristics, then leave it on the cistern for
the next visitor to find.

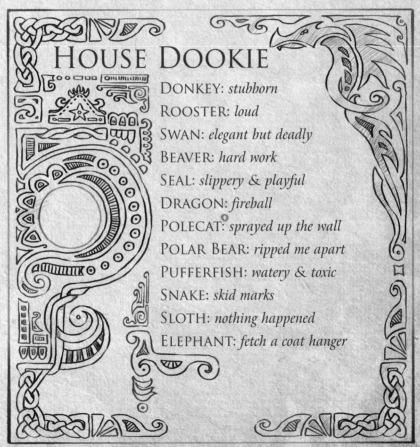

HOUSE DOOKIE

DONKEY: *stubborn*

ROOSTER: *loud*

SWAN: *elegant but deadly*

BEAVER: *hard work*

SEAL: *slippery & playful*

DRAGON: *fireball*

POLECAT: *sprayed up the wall*

POLAR BEAR: *ripped me apart*

PUFFERFISH: *watery & toxic*

SNAKE: *skid marks*

SLOTH: *nothing happened*

ELEPHANT: *fetch a coat hanger*

BATHROOM TILES

How can you cut up this rectangle, so that you can rearrange
the pieces to form one large square?

WALKING ON WATER

The Lady of the Lake rose out of the water and startled Merlin, who
was palely loitering on the bank, soaking up the summer afternoon sun.
'Merlin, a mighty augury is laid,' intoned the watery woman. The wizard
grunted impatiently, for he wanted to be alone with his thoughts.
'I bet you fifty gold coins I can walk across the surface of the lake without
using any magic.'

'Hush thee, poor maiden, and be still!' replied Merlin, for he knew that
without conjuring this was an impossibility. 'I accept your challenge.'

'Then let us meet again at this very spot in six months' time. Or would
you prefer to spare yourself the embarrassment and pay me now?'

How did the Lady win her bet?

WEIGHING BEARS

Answer this question as quickly as you can. Ready? A brown bear weighs
60 shekels more than a black bear. Their combined weight is 120 shekels.

How many shekels does a brown bear weigh?

CIRCLE OF SKULLS

Several human skulls are arranged in a circle. They are evenly spaced and the 8th skull is directly opposite the 20th skull.

How many skulls are there in the circle?

UNBREAKABLE
TOILET PAPER TRICK

Toilet paper advertisements are always banging on about the softness and durability of their product, but this little trick invests it with superhuman qualities (but then, you already knew that didn't you, because, let's face it, toilet paper isn't human). Attach a single sheet of toilet paper to the end of a toilet roll tube with a rubber band. Show the toilet roll to a friend and then throw down the gauntlet:

'I'll wager I can place items into this toilet roll tube that will make it impossible for you to break the tissue paper by pressing on the end.'

If they accept your challenge, simply hold the tube vertically with the paper at the bottom, then fill the tube with rice. When the tube is full, they won't be able to break the tissue by pressing on the rice.

SOAP
SCULPTURE

Soap is a wonderful carving medium; it's really satisfying to work with, smooth and pliable, yet hard enough that you can create some very detailed and intricate carving, limited only by your imagination. For the best results, pick up a cheap 12-chisel wood carving set from eBay.

1. Use ivory soap, which is more moist than ordinary soap and therefore less brittle.

2. Draw the outline of your sculpture on the soap using a marker pen. Choose something simple for your first attempt, like a fish or a heart. Think about how you want the finished piece to feel in your hand, rather than focusing solely on its physical appearance, because touch is very important in sculpture.

3. Using a steak knife, carefully cut around the outline to get the basic shape. Take your time, and apply gentle pressure, otherwise the soap will fracture and crumble. Carefully whittle away all the unwanted pieces.

Make the cutting movements away from you, so that if the knife slips it won't cause an injury.

4. When you've got the basic flat shape, start to smooth off the edges, to round the sculpture out. The steak knife will leave some unwanted serrations, so use a smooth-bladed knife to scrape the surface of the soap until it's smooth, even shiny.

5. When you're satisfied with the smooth, three-dimensional shape, use your chisels to create any finer details (e.g. if you were carving a fish, these would be the eyes, gills, tail and fin lines). If you don't have chisels you can use the tip of a knife.

TOILET ROLL
TELEKINESIS TRICK

Place two toilet roll tubes side by side on a table with the open ends facing you.

Tell your audience that you possess the power of telekinesis and that you will prove this by making the tubes repel each other and move across the table. But first, you must channel your psychic energy through meditation.

Open your hands so they are flat, with fingers touching, palms facing the table. Place your hands just above the toilet roll tubes, purse your lips and start humming.

Spend at least a minute building up a resonant hum. Make the hum grow in volume and intensity as you focus intently on the tubes below you, then lower your head as you suddenly raise the pitch and channel the air through your lips where the tubes meet (the noise of the air will be drowned out by your loud humming).

The blast of air will send the tubes flying apart. If you follow the movement with each hand, it will look as if you are moving them with your mind.

EXERCISES
FOR
EFFECTIVE
ELIMINATIONS

Just because you've been defecating your entire life
doesn't mean you're doing it right. In common with
many mammals, human beings are designed to squat.
In fact, more than 3 billion people in the world
still squat when they lay rope, but in the West we have
built thrones that are great for sanitation but do
our sphincters a grave disservice.

ᐧRAISE YOUR KNEESᐧ

When you sit on a toilet your rectum bends like a banana and creates a kink where it meets the Puborectalis Muscle. But when you squat the kink levels out to create a nearly vertical pipeline. So one way to improve your toilet position is to place something underneath your feet to raise your knees into a squat.

ᐧABDOMEN PUMPINGᐧ

If you are feeling constipated (usually defined as enjoying three or fewer chuds in one week), sucking in your abdomen can really get things moving. Sit up a little straighter than normal and then quickly suck in your belly as if you were trying to tighten a belt, then relax. Repeat this movement several times with a pumping rhythm, while relaxing your sphincter.

ᐧNEVER RUSH OR STRAINᐧ

It shouldn't need saying, but don't rush or strain. Always take your time and think about relaxing rather than forcing the situation. In fact, do something to take your mind elsewhere, like reading a book. This will actually save you time. Men are especially skilled at this and often get criticized for spending half an hour on one visit, but not only does this prove that men are capable of multitasking, it's much better for their general health and wellbeing.

ᐧSUPINE SQUATᐧ

Another pose that helps constipation is assuming a squat position while lying on your back. Bring your knees up to your chest and rest your hands on your knees, then gently rotate them while keeping your back pressed into the floor. Breathe calmly in and out and enjoy the feeling of your thighs pressing into and massaging your abdomen, while your back relaxes, lengthens and widens.

THE
WINTER–SUMMER
QUIZ

When a buzz goes round the neighbourhood that winter
is coming, are you filled with dread? Does the prospect of
enduring months of cold, damp and dark make you want
to emigrate? Or do you long to ditch the shorts, shades and
sun cream, dress up like a Norwegian fisherman and
cosy up in front of the fire?

1. HOW DO YOU BEST LIKE TO SPEND A SUNDAY AFTERNOON?

a. Popping sunburn blisters.

b. Swimming, surfing, beach volleyball, barbecue.

c. Skiing, snowboarding.

d. Debriding necrotic tissue from your face and toes.

2. WHAT'S YOUR FAVOURITE TYPE OF MUSIC?

a. Carly Rae Jepsen, Ibiza anthems, The Beach Boys.

b. Taylor Swift, Jack Johnson, Mungo Jerry.

c. Lana Del Rey, The Cure, Jimmy Eat World.

d. Dead Can Dance, Autopsy, Cannibal Corpse, Bolt Thrower.

3. HAVE YOU EVER HAD A BRAZILIAN?

a. Several times a year.

b. Yes.

c. If God wanted us to shave he wouldn't have invented hipster beards.

d. No, but I once clubbed a penguin to death with a snow shovel.

4. WHAT IS YOUR BMI?

a. Who's counting?

b. 21 to 24.

c. 25 to 30.

d. 18 to 20 or above 30.

5. WHAT IS YOUR DREAM JOB?

a. Sun bed tester.

b. Bikini model.

c. Ski rep.

d. Ice road trucker.

6. WHICH CREATURE ARE YOU MOST SCARED OF?

a. Polar bear.

b. Arctic wolf.

c. Fire ant.

d. Mosquito.

THE WINTER–SUMMER QUIZ:
RESULTS

MOSTLY A: *Scorpion*

You are a diehard sun worshipper who is more comfortable on a tanning bed than watching a total solar eclipse. The only sun protection factor you require in your life is the rotation of the earth. You are an extrovert who lives in the moment and have few body issues, except that during the winter you can't wear white in case you get mistaken for a traffic cone.

MOSTLY B: *Jackrabbit*

You like to feel at one with nature, so long as the sun is shining and you can top off the day with a barbecue and a six pack in the company of like-minded people. You don't mind flashing a bit of flesh in public, but you're not an exhibitionist and your depilation regime indicates that you are physically and emotionally suited to the warmer climate.

MOSTLY C: *Snow Wolf*

Statistically, you are more likely to have been raised in a high socio-economic group and be called Hugo or Tamsin. You love the snow because every school holiday your parents whisked you off to the family chalet in Laax, where you learned to ski and snowboard from the age of four. If you're male you will definitely have experimented with your facial hair and if you're female, you'll know at least seven people with a clinically diagnosed eating disorder.

MOSTLY D: *Glacier Yeti*

Male or female, you are ideologically opposed to the removal of body hair. You err towards the introverted end of the personality spectrum, so you enjoy hiding from the world with layers of clothing and feral androgenic thatch. You over-consume caffeinated energy drinks, have several body piercings and are saving up for a vivarium.

TOILET ROLL TUBE
SNOWFLAKES

Cut three toilet roll tubes into thirty ringlets, each about 1 cm (0.4 in) wide. You should be able to get ten from each roll. Pinch the ends so the rings form petal shapes and then staple them together to create an intricate snowflake pattern. Cut the rings in half to create the innermost and outermost 'petals'.

Use a small stapler, because although a large office stapler will fit through the rings, it's much harder to manoeuvre. Don't even attempt to use quick-bonding glue because it's too fiddly, reduces the flexibility of the rings (making them harder to shape) and you'll probably stick your fingers together. You can copy the snowflake here or make up your own, so long as you maintain hexagonal symmetry.

POO-JITSU:
HOW TO FEND OFF ATTACK WHILE ON THE THRONE

When you're doing your business, you're vulnerable. You're lower than your opponent and your weight may be so far back that if he lunges at you, you've got nowhere to go. So there are a few really important ways to maximize your chances as your assailant approaches.

These techniques should only be used in an emergency when you cannot avoid confrontation or escape from the situation without using force.

›SHIFT YOUR WEIGHT›

Move your weight forward and position your dominant foot and knee so you're ready to spring to your feet. Even if you don't manage to stand up, this stance will give you a more stable base from which to block his attack with your arms.

›ONE-HANDED SHIRT GRAB›
('THIS SEAT IS TAKEN')

If your assailant pulls this move he'll be in very close, so either bring your leg straight up between his legs and hit him in the groin, or sweep your leg sideways.

›PUNCH TO THE HEAD›

Block with your forearm and sweep his punching arm away from your head by rotating your shoulder. This will send him off balance and he may fall headfirst over your knee, allowing you to grab the back of his leg and pop his knee out over your thigh.

›KICK TO THE HEAD‹

Most people are right footed, so the kick will probably come to your left side. Place your left palm against your temple, and bring your elbow up to protect your face (use your right hand if a left-footed kick comes to your right side). Block and control the kick with your other forearm by sweeping your arm down and across your body,

taking the leg away and turning your opponent off balance. Then stand up explosively, and launch into a series of quick counter punches to your assailant's kidney area.

›USE THE TOILET BRUSH‹

Whenever you are in an unfamiliar bathroom, make a point of locating the toilet brush. As your attacker lunges, jab the brush into his eyes – you couldn't reach them with your arms, but the brush gives you an extra forearm of length.

BOWL
READING

The ancient art of reading the toilet bowl is one of the simplest and most attention-grabbing forms of divination. Only a fool or a knave flushes without looking first. A swift chromatic appraisal will tell you everything you need to know about your state of health.

Various factors have an impact on the colour of your number ones, such as hydration, salt intake, liver function, urinary tract infections, kidney stones, bacteria and how many broad beans you've eaten (too many will turn your urine brown, even black). Next time you've made your bladder gladder, check out what your kidney juice says about you:

NO COLOUR, TRANSPARENT:
You're over-hydrated. Drink a little less water otherwise you risk flushing away the important electrolytes from your body.

PALE YELLOW:
You're normally hydrated and healthy. If you peed into a bottle, you should be able to read the newspaper through it.

DARK YELLOW:
You're still within the normal range, but you need to drink some water. If you wait until you're thirsty or have a headache, it's already too late.

BRIGHT YELLOW:
The most likely explanation is you've been taking vitamin supplements.

Colour Code

Amber or Honey:
You are very dehydrated. Drink three cups of water.

Orange:
You are very dehydrated. If it's the morning, it could just be because you've not had a drink for eight hours and your kidneys have been working hard while you were asleep. However, if it persists during the day even after drinking lots of fluids it could indicate a high sodium intake or imbalance, or you might have eaten too many carrots or sweet potatoes. Orange urine can also be a sign of jaundice, typically caused by a blocked bile duct. See your doctor if you are concerned.

Syrup/Brown Mud:
You are dangerously dehydrated and may have liver disease.

Pink to Reddish:
If you've eaten beetroot or blackberries or your haemorrhoids are giving you trouble, don't worry. Otherwise you may have kidney stones or a urinary tract infection, or strenuous exercise may have irritated the bladder lining.

Cloudy:
You may have a bacterial infection. If the problem persists, see a doctor.

BOAT LADDER

A boat's ladder has eight rungs, spaced 30 cm (12 in) apart. The bottom rung is 45 cm (18 in) from the water. The tide is rising at 20 cm every 30 minutes. How many rungs will be under water in two hours' time?

BULLION HEIST

Robbers break into the Queen's treasury and steal thirty bars of gold bullion. They make their getaway by boat, but as they are crossing the lake a fierce storm hits them. Their boat is taking in water, so they throw half the bullion overboard to lighten their load. What happens to the water level in the lake? Does it go up, down or stay the same?

KING OR QUEEN?

A king and queen sit next to each other on separate thrones. 'I am a queen' says the monarch with pink hair. 'I am a king' says the monarch with blue hair. At least one of them is lying. What colour of hair do the king and queen really have?

CLIMB THROUGH A
TOILET ROLL TUBE

There are still plenty of people on this planet who don't know how to do this simple trick and there are gullible new dupes being born every second. Maybe you're one of them. What would you think if someone told you they could walk through a toilet roll tube, while keeping it in one piece?

Would you bet money that they were talking utter feculence?

Well, here's what you do:

1. Cut the tube lengthways and open it out to form a rectangle. It's still in one piece!

2. Fold in half lengthways.

3. Cut along the dotted lines.

4. Open up the cardboard into one giant ring and step through it.

IMPOSSIBLE
TOILET ROLL TUBE TRICK

Here's another little cutting trick that looks impossible.

1. Cut the tube lengthways and open it out to form a rectangle.

2. Cut along the dotted lines.

3. Pick up the cardboard and turn your left hand away from you through 180 degrees to get this: impossible?

47

MAKE TOILET PAPER DREADLOCKS

Dreadlocks are the ideal accoutrement for any sedentary incumbent, since they're reassuringly traditional, yet contemporary. Here's how to create stylish torsades that will keep you amused and entertained while you do your business.

Typically, this artisan craft is quite labour intensive, but a week of bathroom visits should supply you with enough dreads to fashion your own alluring hairpiece that is both functional and decorative, handmade with care and passion. Try experimenting with different coloured strips of toilet paper – greens, blues, creams – since many dreadlocks combine a variety of different hair shades and textures.

1. Take a roll of toilet paper in your dominant hand and wrap about twenty sheets around your other hand in one continuous rolling action.

2. Ease the paper off your hand and while it is still in a roll, cut into three equal strips.

3. Now you need to twist each strip to form toilet paper yarn. Start at one end and just roll the paper towards you as you pass it between the index fingers and thumbs of each hand. It helps to lick your fingers occasionally to give you better grip. Keep twisting and feeding the yarn from one hand to the other until you reach the other end. Then repeat with the other two strips.

4. Knot the three pieces of yarn at one end and then carefully plait them together: cross the right strand over the middle strand. Now the right strand has become the middle and the middle is the right strand. Next, cross the left strand over the new middle strand so it becomes the new middle and so on. Keep plaiting until you run out of yarn.

5. Congratulations! You have made your first toilet paper dreadlock. You just need another nineteen and you're good to go.

THREE TOILET ROLL
PRANKS

HIDING SPIDER

Unroll the toilet paper until you reach the fourth sheet, then carefully separate the two layers and draw a spider on the bottom one with a black ballpoint pen, paying special attention to the shape and orientation of the legs. Then roll the paper back up again.

This half-perceived image, obscured by the translucent toilet paper, should achieve the greatest realism and scare factor. Your victim will think there's a spider trapped (and possibly squashed) in between the layers.

PHANTOM LOG

Soak two toilet roll tubes in warm water until they are dark brown and soften slightly.

Tear the cardboard into small irregular pieces each about the size of a regular postage stamp.

Collect all the pieces and while they are still wet, squash them together in your hands to form a stool shape, fattest in the middle and tapering to a slight point at either end.

Leave the log on the toilet seat, hide and wait for the screams.

GLOWING EYES

Cut eye holes in the centre of four or five toilet roll tubes, then place a glow stick in each and wedge them into some bushes at dusk to scare passers-by.

TOILET PAPER
DOODLING

Toilet paper doodling won't win you a MacArthur Fellowship or the Man Booker Prize, but it exercises the right side of your brain and it's a great way to 'pay it forward' with the minimum of effort. Whether you're painting the ceiling of the Sistine Chapel or doodling a cartoon or abstract design on a small sheet of tissue paper, the same seven aesthetic principles apply: balance, movement, rhythm, pattern, contrast, emphasis and unity.

BALANCE

Balance is the distribution of the visual weight of the elements, colours and textures of your design. It gives a pleasing feeling of equilibrium and is often the key to your piece either looking really good or just 'meh'. In the hands of a grandmaster, a complete lack of balance, unity or technique can create a work so monumentally flawed that it becomes a masterpiece. The greatest example of this is *Lucy in the Field with Flowers*, the founding work of the world-famous Museum of Bad Art in Dedham, Massachusetts, USA. Google it now!

MOVEMENT

Movement is the suggestion or illusion of motion and/or action and it relates to how the elements within the design interact in space over time. An arresting visual image usually includes motion which guides the eye.

RHYTHM

Rhythm is the repetition or alternation of different quantities or conditions. It can create balance and a sense of movement in your design and establish pattern and texture. It engages the viewer by activating space and creating mood. Experiment with different kinds of rhythm: regular, flowing, progressive, alternating and random.

PATTERN

Repetition can be created with
the recurrence of a single element;
pattern is a combination of elements
or shapes repeated in a recurring and
regular arrangement.

CONTRAST

This is the difference in colour, light
and even subject matter between parts
of an image.

EMPHASIS

Think about which parts of
the design you wish to stand
out from the rest. Remember
the little girl with the red coat
in *Schindler's List*? That's a
memorable use of contrast to
produce emphasis, but you
could achieve the same
effect by breaking a
pattern or rhythm.

UNITY

This is probably the most important
design principle and also the most
intangible. It can roughly be summed
up as the sum of the parts being greater
than the whole.

So what are you waiting for?
Get doodling!

RAVEN DIVIDERS

The Yeoman Warders at the Tower of London have arranged nine perches in three rows, but they also need to keep the ravens physically separated. How can they achieve this using just two square dividers?

AXE MEN DUO

Fromondin and Adranus are the quickest axe men in the business. Between them they hold the World Record for beheading: together, they decapitated a crowd of traitors in eight minutes. However, one of the axe men is quicker than his partner. If it would have taken Fromondin twelve minutes to decapitate the same crowd, on his own, how long would it have taken Adranus, if that day Fromondin had called in sick?

DOUBLET PUZZLES

Here are three doublet puzzles. You must transform the left word into the right word in several steps. In each step you can only change one letter and it must form a new word (not a proper name).

For example: COLD » *Cord* » *Card* » *Ward* » WARM

GIVE » ___ » ___ » ___ » TAKE

HEAD » ___ » ___ » ___ » ___ » TAIL

WORK » ___ » ___ » ___ » ___ » ___ » PLAY

CUSTARD CREAM
& TOOTHPASTE PRANK

A regular bathroom cabinet is chock full of items that are ideal for pranking. Toothpaste can work wonders for your smile without going anywhere near your mouth.

Carefully prise apart the two halves of a Custard Cream biscuit or an Oreo using a knife. Scrape away the cream filling and replace with an equal amount of toothpaste. Gently press the halves back together and put the booby-trapped biscuit at the top of the packet. Wait for the screams.

BABY OIL TOILET SEAT

The simplest pranking classics are rarely surpassed.

Pour baby oil into your palm and then rub it onto a toilet seat, making sure you cover every bit of it equally so you end up with a clear uniform shine. Then listen at the door and enjoy!

SEVEN
PARADOXES

If you eat plenty of fibre and drink adequate fluids, but you still relish a bathroom challenge, look no further than these seven classic thought experiments that have been boggling greater minds than yours for millennia.

1. THE OMNIPOTENCE PARADOX

An omnipotent deity must, by definition, be able to do anything, otherwise it wouldn't be omnipotent. So it must be able to do or create something that would challenge its own unlimited power. If this deity created a stone too heavy for it to lift, this suggests the deity's strength has limits, rendering it fallible and challenging its omnipotence. Even an all-powerful being could not resolve this paradox. Maybe the concept of omnipotence is itself paradoxical, intrinsically containing as it does the seeds of its own destruction.

2. SORITES PARADOX

Imagine you came home to find a heap of sand sitting in the bath, piled up to the ceiling. Now, you surely agree that removing a single grain from this heap of sand would not make it any less of a heap. But if you continued to remove one grain at a time, eventually your bath would contain a single grain of sand, which is definitely not a 'heap'. So, at what precise point did your heap turn into a non-heap?

3. A CURE FOR BALDNESS?

If sand in the bath has made you scratch your head or pull out your hair, consider the same paradox in terms of baldness. A man with a full head of hair could lose one hair without going bald. The loss of a single hair could never turn a non-bald man bald. So why are some men bald?

4. ZENO'S ARROW PARADOX

For motion to occur, an object must change the position which it occupies. An arrow in flight moves from the archer to its target. However, in any one instant the arrow can't move to where it is not, because there is no time in which to do this; it can't move to where it is, because it's already there. So if all the separate instants that constitute motion are all motionless, motion must be impossible.

5. ALWAYS TELL THE TRUTH

Sometimes, telling the truth just isn't possible. The next time someone tells you that honesty is always the best policy, ask them this:

'Is "No" your answer to this question?'

If they say 'Yes' they will be lying; if they answer 'No' they will also be lying.

6. UNEXPECTED HANGING

A judge sentences a prisoner to death and tells him that his hanging will take place on one day during the week but take him by surprise. The prisoner reasons that it won't happen on Friday, because, being the last possible day, it wouldn't be a surprise. Then he rules out Thursday for the same reason – and then Wednesday, Tuesday and Monday. To his great surprise, he was executed on Wednesday.

And finally ...

7. TRUE OR FALSE?

The sentence that follows this sentence is false.
The sentence that precedes this sentence is true.

CONQUERING
THE WORLD

Back in the days when a large army, a high wall and a flag were all you needed to lay claim to territory, a dim-witted king set a challenge for his three most distinguished scientists.

'I want to expand my kingdom. I want you to wall off the largest amount of the earth's surface, using the fewest bricks.'

The first scientist suggested a giant square; the second suggested a giant triangle. The third scientist was a mathematician so he made the correct suggestion. The stupid king sent him to prison for his insolence.

What did the third scientist propose?

BORDER CROSSING
SMUGGLER

A notorious smuggler arrives at the border of the kingdom carrying three large sacks on his horse. The border guard stops him and demands to know what's in the bags.

'Sand,' answers the man. The guard replies, 'I'll be the judge of that.'

The guard snatches the bags and cuts them open. Sand pours out. The guard scoops up the sand, puts it in new sacks and sends the smuggler on his way.

A week later the smuggler reaches the border again, with three sacks. The guard cuts them open and finds only sand, and sends him on his way.

This happens every week for a year but the smuggler never gets caught.

What is he smuggling?

MAKE AN OWL CALLER
FROM A TOILET ROLL TUBE

If you run out of toilet paper and need to summon an owl to bring
you a new roll, simply make an improvised owl caller with the toilet roll tube.
Before you begin, shuffle to your study with your trousers round your ankles
to fetch a stapler, craft knife and tape.

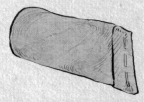

*1. Press one end flat,
staple it closed and seal with tape.*

*2. Press the other end flat,
at right-angles to the first, staple it
closed and seal with tape. You now have
a hollow triangular shape.*

*3. Make a clean and precise triangular
hole at one end using the craft knife.*

*4. Fold the edge underneath
and tape.*

Place the instrument against your bottom lip so that the triangle hole is pointing
towards you. Blow across the top of the hole to summon your toilet paper delivery
owl. Bear in mind that if it's daylight, the bird will probably be asleep.

IMPROVEMENT NOUN GRID

Do you waste hours of your life on the loo thinking about nothing in particular? Well all that's about to change. Here is a list of 42 objects. Pick just one and think about how you can creatively IMPROVE it. This could be the very first step you take to becoming a multi-millionaire inventor and entrepreneur.

Iron	Zipper	Lace	Bookmark	Mp3 Player	Broccoli
Hose Pipe	Playing Card	Wagon	Shampoo	Rug	Cup
Hammer	Fake Flowers	Video Games	Shoe Lace	Deodorant	Mop
Box	Carrots	Sketch Pad	Chocolate	Stapler	Soy Sauce
Doll	Candle	Conditioner	Brandy	Cork	Mirror
Clamp	Purse	Chair	Drawer	CD	Piano
Tyre Swing	Bow	Television	Sticky Note	USB Drive	Bowl

WHO? WHAT? WHEN? WHERE? WHY? HOW?

Deliver	Sneeze	Name	Overflow	Heap	Suffer
Fool	Smile	Care	Explode	Cover	Clip
Invent	Wonder	Soothe	Join	Agree	Sigh
Enter	Squeak	Signal	Wreck	Spare	Satisfy
Sip	Shade	Chew	Knit	Raise	Trace

Now pick three objects from the first sheet and two verbs from the second, then tie them together in a dramatic scenario by answering the questions Who? What? When? Where? Why? How? For example, if you picked candle, drawer, broccoli, explode and overflow you might do this:

Who: *Chef*

What (happened): *exploded*

When: *at night*

Where: *kitchen*

Why: *brandy overflowed in drawer*

How: *was heating broccoli on a spoon over a candle*

MAKE A WEDDING RICE SHOOTER
FROM A TOILET ROLL TUBE

Party poppers are great fun but they cause litter and if you're at a wedding you want to throw rice. Armed with a toilet roll you can spray rice at the happy couple. It's a happy coincidence that a toilet roll tube is just the right size to fit two party poppers, side by side.

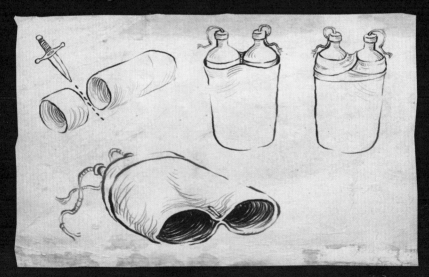

1. Cut about 2.5 cm (1 in) off one end of the tube.

2. Fit the party poppers snugly inside at one end and seal with tape so no air can escape out of the bottom.

3. Squeeze the other end so it forms a double-barrel shape, then staple in place.

4. Add a handful of rice and you're ready to fire. Make sure you aim straight up in the air and not at anyone's face.

TEN COOL USES FOR A
BAR OF SOAP

Soap is one of the most underrated items that we use every day without thinking about how it works or how many other ways we can use it. Humans have been making soap for thousands of years – the earliest written soap recipe dates back to Ancient Babylonia, 4,800 years ago. It cleans things because one end of a soap molecule is hydrophilic (attracted to water) and the other is lipophilic (attracted to oil), so it binds to dirt, oil and bacteria and then when you rinse it away, the hydrophilic ends of the molecule follow the water, taking the impurities and bacteria with them.

If that wasn't incredible enough, here are some other uses you probably didn't know about:

1. Rub soap on metal to provide lubrication. Nails and screws will go into wood more easily if they are rubbed with soap first. Rubbing soap on a metal saw blade will prevent it from sticking to the wood. Rusty zippers glide smoothly when rubbed with soap.

2. Before gardening, scrape your fingernails on a bar of soap. This will stop dirt building up under your nails and it can easily be washed away.

3. Dissolve a little soap in a bottle and spray it on the underside of leaves to deter bugs.

4. Use the same spray around the house to deter spiders and insects.

5. Rub soapy water on a gas pipe joint. If it bubbles, you know you have a leak. If you have a gas barbecue, use this method to check for leaks, especially where the regulator is attached to the gas canister.

6. Rub soap on the bottom of cooking pans so when you cook over an open fire you can wash away the soot more easily afterwards.

7. Rub spectacle lenses with soapy fingers then polish to stop them from steaming up in cold weather.

8. Rub an insect bite with soap to relieve the itching and pain and keep the wound clean.

9. Put bits of soap in an old pair of tights and hang them from trees and plants to deter deer.

10. Use soap to mark up a seam when sewing, because it washes out more easily than tailor's chalk.

BOOLEAN LOGIC
PUZZLES

The five puzzles on this page involve knights and knaves. Some also contain talking ravens. All you need to know is that knights always tell the truth, knaves always lie and talking ravens can either lie or tell the truth.

1. Lambin the Eager and Ranulph the Powerful are walking down the road. Lambin turns to Ranulph and says, 'We are both knaves.' *Is he lying or telling the truth?*

2. Borin the Great and Aldus the Loner are sitting in a walled garden. Aldus says to Borin, 'We are the same,' and Borin replies, 'We are opposites.' *Who is lying?*

3. Randal the Persistent and Tristan the Dragonheart each guard a door. One leads to Heaven, the other leads to Hell. One of them is a knave and the other is a knight. *What question must you ask to determine which is the door to Heaven?*

4. Wiscard the Harbinger says, 'I am a knight.' Guillame the Timid replies, 'That is true.' Helewisa of the Lake says, 'I am a raven.' *If one of them is a knight and one a knave, is the raven lying or telling the truth?*

5. Philbert the Reckless says, 'I am not a raven.' Renard the Honourable replies, 'You are correct.' Salamon of the Mountain lies, 'You are both lying.' *Is Philbert a knight, knave or raven?*

WINTER IS COMING

Two knights, who had been riding all day through a huge forest, finally reached a clearing where they stopped, pitched camp, lit a fire and spent the night. When they woke in the morning there was a thick covering of snow on the ground, but they also discovered lots of footsteps and hoof prints in the snow. They hadn't met another soul for one hundred miles. They had stayed in their tent all night and the horses had been securely tethered. How did the footprints appear?

MURDER IN THE DESERT

Three princes were walking across a desert kingdom. The first and second princes both hated the third prince. The first prince secretly poisoned the water bottle of the third prince. The second prince made a hole in the third prince's water bottle, unaware that the water had already been poisoned. Three days later the third prince died of thirst. Who was the murderer?

THE INHERITANCE RACE

An old king has a son and a daughter. He sets them a challenge to see who will inherit the throne, sending them on a race to a distant city. The one whose horse is slowest is to win the kingdom.

The siblings set off but they spend the first week trying to outdo each other with their tardiness and lack of direction. Luckily, they meet an old wise hermit who tells them how to resolve the stalemate. Then the prince and princess jump back on their horses and sprint for the finish line.

What did the hermit tell them to do?

MAKE A TOILET ROLL TUBE
CROSSBOW

YOU WILL NEED:

9 sheets of A4 paper, 3 small emery boards,
a toilet roll tube, dental floss, pencil, craft knife and tape.

1. First make the bow arms. Take four sheets of paper and fold them in half along the long side. Cut along the crease so you have two strips of 4 sheets.

2. Roll each strip of four tightly around a pencil to make a cylinder, then tape.

3. Cut 4 cm (1.5 in) off each end of one of the emery boards and then stick one of these short pieces right inside one end of each paper tube.

4. Stick a full-size emery board halfway into the other end of each paper tube, at right angles to the shorter pieces of emery board.

5. Bend the paper tubes at the point where the emery boards meet.

6. Make the body of the crossbow by rolling five sheets of A4 paper tightly around a pencil and securing with tape.

7. Tape the short side of the bow arms to one end of the body.

8. Make a hole in the end of the emery board at the end of each bow arm and attach the dental floss string. Make sure the arms are bent at about 45 degrees when you attach the string, so it's already under tension.

9. Pull the string back until the string and arms form a diamond shape. Mark the corner of the string and make a slit all the way through the body at this point with a craft knife. Cut a 4 cm (1.5 in) piece of emery board in two and stick one of them into the hole to make the trigger.

10. Cut about 4 cm (1.5 in) off the end of a toilet roll tube, then roll this end around a pencil and tape to make a small guiding tube for your pencil arrow. Attach it to the front of the crossbow, load up your pencil and you're ready to shoot.

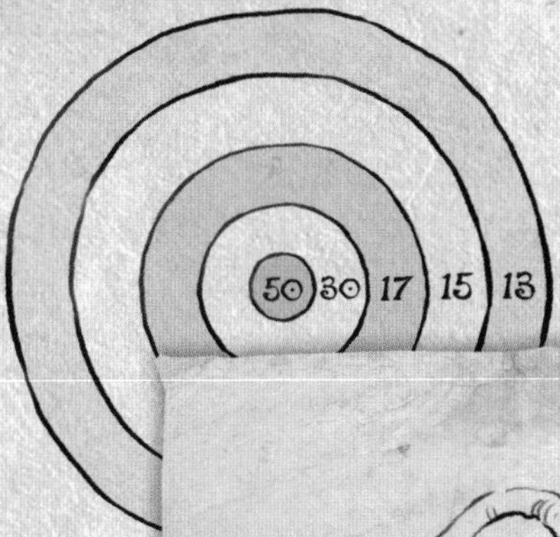
50
30
17
15
13

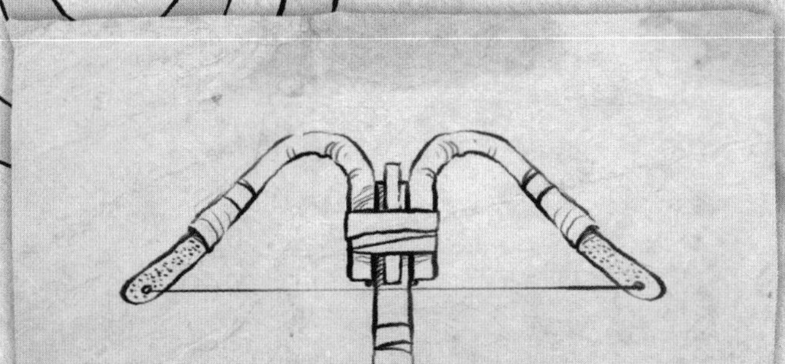

TIE A ROPE AROUND THE
WORLD

If you could tie a long rope around the earth at the equator, it would need to be 40,075 km (24,900 miles) long. Now imagine you wanted a rope that would go around the earth at the equator, raised 1 metre (39.37 in) above the ground.

How much longer would the rope have to be to achieve this?

THRONE WARS

King Guimart and Queen Claramunda couldn't agree about who was the most important. The king demanded that the queen be seated behind him at court, but the queen insisted her throne be placed in front of his. How did they eventually resolve the matter to their mutual satisfaction?

DROP A TOILET ROLL, AMAZE YOUR FRIENDS,
CONFOUND YOUR ENEMIES

Even more impressive than throwing an axe, dropping a toilet roll so it lands on its end every time will not only win you bar bets, it may save your life (because every second spent on this trick is time not spent landing an axe in your frontal lobes).

Hold the toilet roll about five degrees from horizontal and about 30 cm (12 in) from the floor or table top. Let go. The roll will bounce on its side and then magically leap up onto its end.

LEAVE A TOILET ROLL BOW

There are lots of elaborate ways to primp your toilet roll with bows and whistles on, but the method shown here is by far the easiest and the quickest, plus it looks great as well.

1. Remove a four-sheet strip of toilet paper from the roll.

2. Fold it in half from bottom to top so that it becomes two strips on top of one another.

3. Cut the top strip into a ribbon shape, tapered at the end.

4. Gather up the front strip into a concertina with six or seven separate folds, using both hands and working with your fingertips in the centre of the sheet.

5. Hold the middle of the concertina between the index finger and thumb of one hand as you roll the ribbon several times around the middle of the bow.

6. Tuck the end into the back of the bow.

7. Attach the bow to the toilet roll using a small decorative pin.

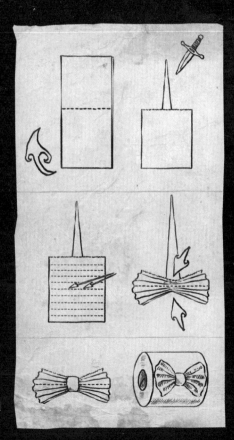

BATH
SPONGE BALLS TRICK

Who doesn't love playing with their balls in the bathroom?
First you need to make two sponge balls and then
hollow one of them out:

TO MAKE YOUR BALLS

1. Cut two large cubes of equal size out of your sponge.

2. Cut off the eight corners and then keep cutting and rotating the sponge to create a rough ball shape. Don't worry about making a perfect sphere. In fact, the trick will work better if you end up with two slightly craggy boulders, disguising the join when you hide one ball inside the other.

3. Using a craft knife, hollow out one of the balls. The easiest way is to cut a cylinder, then turn it inside out so that it looks like a mushroom and cut away the 'stalk'. Then shave off more of the insides while it is inside out.

4. Squeeze the solid ball, stuff it inside the hollow ball and let go. The two sponges should now look like a single craggy ball. You are ready to perform your trick.

THE TRICK

1. Show the ball to your victim and tell them to watch closely as you perform your magic.

2. Briefly rub your hands together, so that you end up with one ball in each hand, then hold your closed fists in front of you ready for your victim to pick where they think the ball ended up.

3. No matter which hand they choose, you will always be able to open the other hand to reveal a ball.

MAKE TOILET ROLL TUBE
GARGOYLES

French paper artist Junior Fritz Jacquet knows better than anyone the importance of saving toilet roll tubes and ensuring no one in his household throws one away again. Ever. He turns them into expressive faces that convey an eerie mixture of humour and tristesse. Then he coats them in shellac and paints them until they resemble clay, bronze, fabric ... anything but the humble cardboard from which they originated.

According to his bio, 'He explores and experiments with folding and crumpling techniques, innovating, with his fingers, methods still undiscovered to create forms and craft poetic objects that visually enhance any surrounding.'

1. Position a reading light to your left or right to gain maximum contrast as you work so the facial features gain the greatest definition.

2. Humans are expert at facial recognition. Who hasn't as a child stared at the creases, shades and patterns in their bedroom curtains or ceiling and spotted faces where there are none? Trust this skill and allow your instincts to guide you as you improvise with the cardboard. A crease can quickly become a furrowed brow, a nose or squinting eyes if you relax and allow your incredible fusiform gyrus to lead the way. Oh, that? It's one of the many

important bits of your brain that helps you to see, recognize and remember faces. And you will have to improvise because these little cardboard tubes are more stubborn than you think, so they will constantly frustrate your artistic vision by refusing to bend and crease to your will.

3. You can only learn about a material by working with it. The simpler something looks, the more likely it is to be technically complex and fastidiously constructed. So you will need lots of patience and a willingness to improvise, experiment and make lots of mistakes.

4. Work from big to small: make the eye sockets, nose, mouth, forehead ridge, etc. before attempting the finer details. However, this doesn't have to be a fixed rule – don't lose out on a detail like a fantastic philtrum or chin dimple if it suddenly springs into view. It could inform the whole piece, so stay alert and flexible.

5. Experiment with a range of tools and techniques to shape the cardboard: cutting, wetting, scoring, creasing, layering, etc.

6. Place or glue small objects inside the roll and then press the cardboard into them to help you achieve clear distinct shapes. For example, you can sculpt a nose around the nose of your pliers, or glue in a pen lid.

7. Use superglue or a hot glue gun to fix areas of the face so that you don't lose them while working on the other features.

Royal Box

The king places a secret message in a box and locks it with his padlock. He gives the box to a messenger with instructions to take it directly to his sister who rules the neighbouring kingdom. She has her own padlock and key, but doesn't own a key to his padlock. So, without breaking the lock or the box, what should the sister do to ensure that she can open the box and read the message, but the messenger can't?

Seven Warriors

Seven warriors are encircled by an enemy army which consists of thousands of bloodthirsty swordsmen. They cannot escape. But they know an important secret. Ancient lore dictates that if they stand in such a way that they form six rows with three warriors standing along each row, the enemy will disperse in terror because of the ancient prophecy: 'Those thrice six from seven conceive, shall mighty armies hew and cleave'. Which configuration should the seven warriors adopt?

Ravine Teaser

Four mammoths plodding along a steep mountain ravine meet four mammoths plodding the other way. The meeting point is too narrow for the mammoths to pass. Mammoths never retreat, but they will climb over each other if there is a mammoth-sized space on the other side.

The two groups of mammoths stop. They are facing each other with exactly one mammoth's width between them.

How can all mammoths pass, allowing both groups to go on their way, without any mammoth reversing?

THE MISSING SWORD

Two warring tribes brokered peace with a wedding. King Armundus, the ruler of one tribe, offered his daughter in marriage to King Wandereye Wilmot, ruler of the other tribe, along with a dowry of 30 falchion swords of the very finest quality, which had been donated by three of the king's richest noblemen. The young bride was so beautiful that when the roving eye of its namesake saw her for the first time he was overcome with gratitude and instructed his servant to return five of the falchion swords as a gesture of his immense satisfaction. But the runtish servant disobeyed his master and only returned three swords, keeping the other two for himself. So now the three noblemen of King Armundus had each donated only nine swords, 27 in total, and the servant had kept two. What happened to the missing sword?

TOILET PAPER SABOTAGE

Carefully separate the two layers of a roll of two-ply toilet paper, tear off the front layer of the first sheet and then pass the rest of the front layer back around the roll so it hangs down behind. Now bring the two layers – one at the front one at the back – together again so the roll looks normal and snip off the bottom so the roll begins with a double layer. Unrolling the toilet paper now becomes a deeply unrewarding experience and it won't be immediately apparent what you've done.

SQUARE SHIELD

A retiring knight decides to make a square card-table top from his old shield. He wants his table to be as large as possible but his saw is blunt and rusty, so he wants to make the fewest possible cuts. He saws the shield into three pieces and turns them into a square, without wasting any of the wood.

How does he do it?

WHAT ARE THE NEXT TWO NUMBERS IN THE SEQUENCE?

16 06 68 88 __ __

MAKE IVORY SOAP MERINGUE

1. Cut a brand new fresh bar of ivory soap into eight pieces and place them on a plate in the microwave oven (don't use old soap).

2. Set the timer for 90 seconds and press Start.

3. Ivory soap is filled with little pockets of air that get hot and expand to make a big fluffy meringue that looks good enough to eat (don't).

SIX SOAP CUBES

How can you arrange six identically sized soap cubes so that each cube touches at least a small part of the faces of the other five cubes (edges and corners don't count).

THE LION AND THE
UNICORN

A lion and a unicorn meet in a forest. The lion lies on Mondays, Tuesdays and Wednesdays and tells the truth on the other days of the week. The unicorn only lies on Thursdays, Fridays and Saturdays. The lion announces: 'Yesterday I was lying.' The unicorn replies, 'So was I.' What day is it?

CHEAP
LODGING

An errant knight rides into the castle on Tuesday and asks the gatekeeper how much it will cost him to sojourn there. The gatekeeper replies, 'One gold coin per night, sir knight.' The knight leaves on Friday morning, satisfied with the excellent hospitality he has received, but he only owes one gold coin. Why?

PRINCE RUPERT'S
CUBE

Is it mathematically possible to make a hole in a cube that is wide enough for a larger cube to pass through, without the smaller cube falling apart?

MAKE A TOILET PAPER
ROSE

If you work in a hotel, adding one of these little beauties to the end of a toilet roll will increase your tips and may even attract return custom. Even if you're just sitting at home, you can tell guests that your housekeeper made it. That's right – they'll think you have a housekeeper, just because you can make flowers out of bog roll. They take seconds to make and it's so easy.

1. Tear off a strip of toilet paper four sheets long.

2. Feed one long edge little by little between your thumb and index finger, twisting the very top edge to form a tiny little rim.

3. Pinch the middle of the left end of the strip in your left hand. Pinch the paper between the finger and thumb of your right hand, about 4 cm (1.5 in) away from your left hand, gather it towards your left hand, then push it into your left hand as you rotate the paper clockwise.

4. Keep pinching, gathering, pushing and rotating until you reach the other end of the strip. Now you have all the paper in your left hand, collected in a spiral shape. It already resembles a rose, but the next step completes the effect.

6. Twist the bottom of the stalk until it is firm and tidy.

5. Pinch the bottom of the stalk in your right hand, then cup the fingers of your left hand at the bottom of the flower and gently push upwards as you squeeze to make a nice compact rose head.

7. You can attach the rose to the toilet paper roll by twisting the front three sheets around to form a piece of yarn, then make a loop and tuck the end underneath. Gently feed the stalk through the loop and tighten the loop to secure the rose.

CONFUCIUS SAY

Create a wise Confucian epigram by choosing a
random word from *A, B, C, A* or *C, A, B, A*.

A

legs	finger	toothbrush	guilt	love
rabbit	elbow	umbrella	happiness	hate
horse	scarf	wheel	time	peace
dog	name	excellence	insanity	desire
jellyfish	egg	freedom	jealousy	disgust
fairy	bucket	gratitude	fame	dignity

B

kicks	answers	prepares	rushes
makes	decorates	worries	squeezes
squashes	divides	promises	carries
scrapes	catches	opens	tastes
finds	stops	follows	suffers

C

curious	organic	numerous	temporary	powerful
overconfident	tearful	breezy	cuddly	red
spurious	intelligent	wise	strong	callous
warm	hungry	wandering	silly	successful
sharp	unwieldy	gentle	bored	cheap
quiet	solid	homeless	fat	lonely

Now spend a few minutes stroking your chin and contemplating
its profound meaning. Here are two examples:

'Gratitude kicks hungry time.'

'Curious happiness worries legs.'

KNIGHT BOOTS

The Green Knight, the Red Knight and the Black Knight meet at a banquet. One is wearing red boots, the second is wearing green boots and the third black boots. One of the knights comments, 'We are all wearing boots that are a different colour to our names.' The man in the green boots replies, 'Yes Sir Red, you are correct.'

What colour of boots is each knight wearing?

FOUR DOORS

Behind one of the doors there is treasure. Only one of the inscriptions is correct.

Can you work out where the treasure is?

| DOOR 1 | DOOR 2 | DOOR 3 | DOOR 4 |

| IT'S BEHIND 2 OR 3 | IT'S BEHIND 1 OR 4 | IT'S IN HERE | IT'S NOT IN HERE |

VANISHING
TOOTHBRUSH TRICK

Dentists believe that all the evil in the world could be overcome if only everyone would pass a thread of waxed nylon between their teeth on a daily basis. So, the next time your dentist evangelizes about the need to floss more regularly, demonstrate that you're the boss by making a toothbrush vanish right in front of their eyes. But practise the trick on the toilet first until it's perfect.

1. Hold the toothbrush in front of you, horizontally, between the index finger, middle finger and thumb of each hand, with your knuckles facing the viewer.

2. Make sure the handle end of the toothbrush is in your dominant hand, because the vanishing effect requires a little dexterity.

3. Count to three, then lift your hands up and down about an inch quickly with a flourish (the internationally accepted distraction technique of amateur magicians the world over). This will disguise your movement of the toothbrush through a

90-degree angle to hide behind your forearm. You press down with your middle finger (which is resting on top of the shaft) and make the toothbrush pivot around your index finger, almost as if you were snapping your fingers to make a clicking noise.

4. To make the toothbrush reappear, place your middle finger underneath the handle and flick your finger back up.

5. It's important to lock your arms to maintain the same distance between your hands while you move the toothbrush.

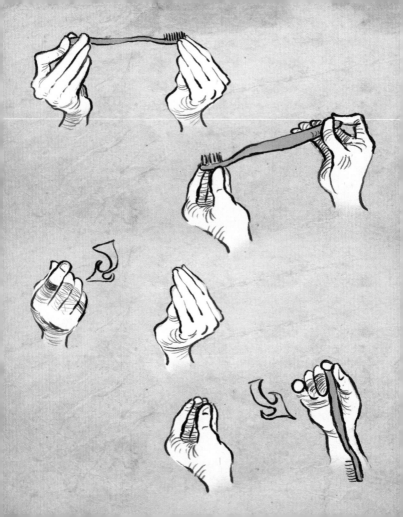

MAKE CHAIN MAIL
WITH POP TABS

The best time to plant a tree is twenty years ago. The second best time is now. The same applies to pop tab chain mail. When you start collecting the thousand or so tabs you'll need for this ambitious venture, you'll never be able to walk down the street again without scanning the floor for aluminium treasure. You'll wistfully recall the dozens of drinks cans you casually tossed aside before chain mail became your top priority. And it will. Which is why this project comes with a giant warning: 'POP TABS CAN TAKE OVER YOUR LIFE – but only if you let them.'

So dream big and remember, a journey of a thousand pop tabs begins with the first can. To paraphrase the hustling Cuban-American visionary, Pitbull: get it started, because if it feels right (you know it feels right), you shouldn't waste any more time.

YOU WILL NEED:

Wire cutters, long nose pliers, staple remover, 1,000 pop tabs.

1. Prepare your pop tabs for assembly. Using the long nose pliers, bend back the square spur (where the tab was attached to the can) and squash it against the side of the tab.

2. Using the wire cutters, make a single cut at the other end.

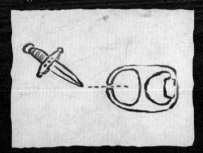

3. Use the staple remover to bend the tab.

4. Repeat steps 1 to 3 one thousand times!

5. Fit them together in rows by attaching two tab handles to the base of the one above.

6. Make a front section and a back section – rectangles of equal size – then join them together at the shoulders and sides. You can't make it out of one giant piece because one side will be upside down and you won't be able to join up the sides.

7. Allow plenty of room for head and arms, because unlike fabric, this chain mail will not stretch. It's advisable to wear a close-fitting T-shirt underneath the chain mail to protect against scratches, so factor that into your design as well.

8. After each session, wash your hands to remove all traces of aluminium (unless you were wearing gloves). But if you're doing this on the loo, you should be washing your hands anyway, right?

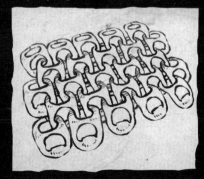

LEVITATE
A SHEET OF
TOILET PAPER

This amazing trick uses no hidden wires or other paraphernalia. It's real levitation using the hidden power of static electricity. Once you know the secret, you'll be able to make a sheet of toilet paper literally float in the air between your hands.

YOU WILL NEED:

Two plastic straws from a fast food restaurant, still in their paper casing.

1. Place a sheet of toilet paper ready on the edge of a table so that half of it is hanging over.

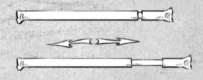

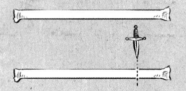

2. Cut around the casing about 3 cm (1 in) from one end of each straw so you get a long piece of casing and a short piece, but don't unwrap the straws. Leave them in the casing.

3. Grip both straws, with the short piece of wrapping, between your teeth.

4. Hold a long piece of casing in each hand and then quickly rub the casing up and down each straw as if you were playing a trombone. This will build up a positive charge on the straw.

and your left index finger on the other. Don't touch the table.

5. Now quickly whip the long casing completely away from the straw, grip a straw in each hand, remove them from your teeth, hold for a count of three and then drop them.

8. Raise your hands to chest level and slowly bring them apart. The sheet of paper will now float like magic for several seconds.

6. The positive charge has now been transferred from the straws to your hands. Keep your hands apart. Don't let them touch or the charge will dissipate.

7. Now pick up the sheet of toilet paper in the middle, with your right index finger on one face

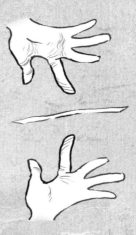

L-SHAPED
INHERITANCE

Queen Thyphainne has an L-shaped kingdom that she wishes to divide equally between her four daughters. Her kingdom is already enclosed by a huge boundary wall, so how many miles of extra wall will she need?

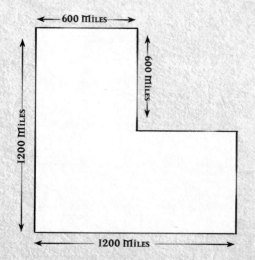

FALCONRY
PUZZLE

King Malcolm Margrave Loyset Bartholomeus Gefroy Isemberd III has three falcons which can catch three mice in three minutes.

How many additional falcons would Malcolm need to catch 100 mice in 100 minutes?

MISSING
FISH

Two fathers went fishing with their sons. The fathers caught two fish each and the two sons caught three fish in total. They returned home that evening with their catch of five fish. If they didn't eat them or throw them back, what happened to the other two?

CONDEMNED TO
DEATH

If you were condemned to death, which of these ancient methods from around the world would give you the best chance of survival?

1. Slowly being sliced to death, having portions of your body removed bit by bit.

2. Suffocated in a room filled with ash (popular in Ancient Persia).

3. Decapitation with a katana sword.

4. Buried in a ditch up to your waist and then stoned.

5. Crushed by having heavy stones placed on your chest (known in France as *peine forte et dure* – 'hard and forceful punishment').

6. Locked in a cage with lions that haven't eaten for five months.

7. Sawed in half at the waist (a method favoured by the Roman Emperor Caligula).

8. Scaphism: Persian torture of being tied naked between two boats in a stagnant pond, covered in honey, then devoured by insects and killed by gangrene.

WOULD YOU
RATHER

1. Change your name to Justin Bieber OR never eat chocolate again?

2. Travel 200 years into the past to visit your ancestors OR travel 200 years into the future to visit your descendants?

3. Go on a two-week vacation anywhere in the world OR get locked in a room with a celebrity of your choice for one hour?

4. Know the date of your death OR the cause of your death?

5. Be richer OR better looking?

6. Lose a leg OR lose your hearing?

7. Always know when someone is lying OR always be able to lie convincingly?

8. Win the lottery OR eradicate world poverty?

9. Eat as much as you like without any negative consequences OR lie as much as you like without any negative consequences?

10. Be the best teacher in the world OR the smartest person in the world?

11. Be stuck on a desert island with someone you can't stand OR be stuck there alone?

12. Be the most talented artist in the world but penniless OR the richest artist in the world but talentless?

13. Memorize any book in one minute OR read minds?

14. Have the best house in a downbeat neighbourhood OR the worst house in an upmarket neighbourhood?

15. Freeze to death OR burn to death?

16. Have a dragon OR be a dragon?

17. Be the best sword fighter in the world OR the best sword maker who ever lived?

18. Smell like a toilet and not know it OR think everyone else smells like a toilet?

19. Have constantly itchy fingers OR constantly sticky fingers?

20. Wear someone else's dirty underwear for a week OR not brush your teeth for a month?

ANSWERS

– PAGE 7 –
PRINCE OR PRINCESS?

There are four possible scenarios: BB, BG, GB, GG, each with a 1 in 4 probability.

If one is a boy, the GG scenario can be discounted, which leaves three scenarios, each with a 1 in 3 probability: BB, BG, GB. So now the probability that one of the children is a girl is 2 in 3 or 66.666 per cent.

POISONED PIES

Yes. At the start, the probability that the King's pie was safe was 1 in 3. He was twice as likely to be holding a poisoned pie than the safe one (it was twice as likely that the safe pie was with either Rosencrantz or Guildenstern). So once it had been established that Rosencrantz's pie was poisoned, Guildenstern's pie becomes the safest bet.

COAT OF ARMS

Rule 1: The number of strings on the harp determines the number of dragons on the next shield.

Rule 2: An even number of dragons face left; an odd number of dragons face right.

– PAGE 8 –
BATHROOM TILES

There are 30 rectangles (because squares are types of rectangle).

MATCHSTICKS & TOILET ROLL

THREE PRIVIES

Turn on switches 1 and 2 and wait for three minutes. Then turn off Switch 2 and run to either the East or the West Turret. If the light is on, he knows this is Switch 1. If the light is off, he should touch the bulb. If it's still warm, it's Switch 2. If it's cold, it's Switch 3. Next he should go to the South Turret (if he's discovered Switch 1 he should run; otherwise he can walk), where he uses the same logic to determine the correct switch, then he can return directly to the North Turret to inform the King because the remaining switch has been discovered by a process of elimination.

– PAGE 15 –
THREE SLAVES BET

No. If the Queen gives two slaves and the King gives nothing back, he loses the bet and must give the Queen one slave. So the King gains a slave for doing nothing. However, if the King wins the bet by giving the Queen three slaves, she must give him one slave. So either way, she stands either to lose a slave or break even.

BURNING ISLAND

They must take about twenty steps to the west, then face east and set light to the trees. The wind will spread the fire to the east and then burn out, leaving them a safe place to stand when the larger fire eventually reaches them.

GUINEVERE'S GRANDMOTHER

Her father's mother is two years older than Guinevere's mother.

– PAGE 18 –
SEVEN ARROWS

1. 15, 15, 15, 15, 15, 15, 13
or
17, 15, 15, 15, 15, 13, 13
or
17, 17, 15, 15, 13, 13, 13
2. Four. 30, 30, 30, 13.

HOW LONG IS THIS JOUSTING TILT?

The length of this tilt is twice the distance from the middle to the end.

HOW MANY DROPS OF WINE?

One. After the first drop the flagon is no longer empty.

– PAGE 32 –
BATHROOM TILES

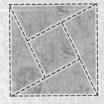

WALKING ON WATER

In six months' time it would be winter and the lake would be frozen.

WEIGHING BEARS

90 shekels.

– PAGE 33 –
CIRCLE OF SKULLS

There are 24 skulls. If the 8th skull is opposite the 20th skull, then the 14th skull must be an equal distance from both of them, since 20 minus 14 = 6 and 14 minus 8 = 6. So the 2nd skull must be opposite the 14th skull.

– PAGE 46 –
BOAT LADDER

None. The boat floats.

BULLION HEIST

When the gold is in the boat it displaces its weight in water, but when it is thrown overboard it only displaces its volume of water, which is less than its weight (we know this because it sinks in water). So the water level goes down.

KING OR QUEEN?

The king has pink hair and the queen has blue hair. If at least one of them is lying, then both of them must be lying.

If the pink-haired monarch saying 'I am a queen' = LIE, then the blue-haired monarch must be the queen, so saying 'I am a king' also = LIE.

If the pink-haired monarch saying 'I am a queen' = TRUE, one must lie, so saying 'I am a king' = LIE, but they can't both be queens, so once again, they are both lying.

– Page 52 –
Raven Dividers

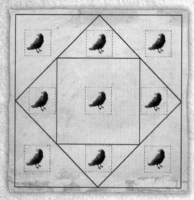

Axe Men Duo

Fromondin could have completed 8/12 of the work in 8 minutes, so Adranus must have done 4/12 = 1/3. Working on his own, Fromondin would have taken 3 x 8 = 24 minutes.

– Page 53 –
Doublet Puzzles

GIVE » GAVE » RAVE » RAKE » TAKE

HEAD » HEAL » TEAL » TELL » TALL » TAIL

WORK » PORK » PORT » PERT » PEAT » PLAT » PLAY

– Page 56 –
Conquering the World

The mathematician suggests building a small circular wall, thus fencing off the entire world apart from a small circle.

Border Crossing Smuggler
Horses.

– Page 62 –
Boolean Logic Puzzles

1. Lying – if he is a knave, then saying he is a knave is telling the truth.

2. They can't both be liars because Aldus would be telling the truth; they can't both be telling the truth because their statements contradict each other. So Aldus must be a liar and Borin tells the truth.

3. 'What would the other guard say is the door to Heaven?' Whichever door the guard points to is the door to Hell. If the guard is telling the truth, he truthfully reports the other guard's lie; if the guard lies, he lies about the other guard's

truthful statement. Either way, you should choose the other door.

4. Truth – there are only two possible scenarios:

a) Wiscard = knight, Guillame = raven telling the truth, Helewisa = knave

b) Wiscard = knave, Guillame = knight, Helewisa = raven telling the truth

5. Philbert can only be a lying raven or a knight. If he is a lying raven, Renard is either a lying raven or a knave, making Salamon's statement true. But we know Salamon is lying, so Philbert must be a knight.

– PAGE 63 –
WINTER IS COMING

It had already snowed before they arrived at the clearing.

MURDER IN THE DESERT

The second prince is the murderer. The third prince died of thirst, so all the poisoned water must have leaked out of the bottle before he had the chance to drink any.

THE INHERITANCE RACE

He told them to swap horses. This means they can now race to the city to try to beat their own horse and inherit the kingdom.

– PAGE 66 –
TIE A ROPE AROUND THE WORLD

The circumference of a circle $= 2\pi$ x radius. If the radius increases by 1 metre (39.37 in) the circumference increases by 2π x 1 metre = 6.284 metres (20.62 feet), so the rope would only need to be 6.284 metres (20.62 feet) longer.

THRONE WARS

Place the thrones back to back.

– PAGE 72 –
ROYAL BOX

She locks the box with her padlock and sends it back to the king. The king then removes his padlock and sends it back to her. She unlocks her padlock, opens the box and reads the message.

SEVEN WARRIORS

RAVINE TEASER

A mammoth from one side moves forward into the gap. A mammoth from the other side climbs over him into the new gap. Then a mammoth from the first side climbs over two mammoths (the one who's just climbed, plus one of his own companions) to reach the gap, followed by one from the other side climbing over three, and so on.

– PAGE 73 –
THE MISSING SWORD

There is no missing sword. The knave kept two swords out of a total of 27 and his king kept 25. You have to work up from 25 rather than down from 30, otherwise it seems paradoxical.

– PAGE 74 –
SQUARE SHIELD

WHAT ARE THE NEXT TWO NUMBERS IN THE SEQUENCE?

__ __ 88 89 90 91

– PAGE 75 –
SIX SOAP CUBES

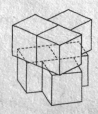
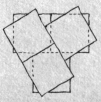

Top View

The Lion and the Unicorn

Thursday. The lion can only make his statement on Monday (lying about telling the truth on Sunday) or Thursday (telling the truth about lying on Wednesday). The unicorn can only make his statement on Thursday (lying about telling the truth on Wednesday) or Sunday (telling the truth about lying on Saturday).

Cheap Lodging

The knight's horse is called Tuesday and he arrived at the castle on Thursday.

Prince Rupert's Cube

Yes. The mathematical problem was posed by one of the founders of The Royal Society, Prince Rupert of the Rhine, during the seventeenth century. It was subsequently solved by English mathematician John Wallis, and improved further one hundred years later by Dutch mathematician Pieter Nieuwland. Both men showed that a slightly larger cube can pass through a smaller one.

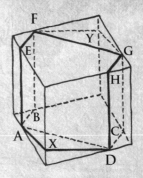

– Page 79 –
Knight Boots

The knight with the green boots must be the Black Knight because he addresses the Red Knight by name. He can't be the Green Knight because the boots can't match his name. So the Red Knight can only be wearing black boots and the Green Knight must be wearing red boots.

Four Doors

If the treasure is behind Door 1, then both 2 and 4 are true.
If the treasure is behind Door 2, then both 1 and 4 are true.
If the treasure is behind Door 3, then 1, 3 and 4 are true.

– PAGE 79 CONT–

If the treasure is behind Door 4, then all the signs are false, except for that on Door 2.

So the treasure is behind Door 4, because it's the only solution in which only one inscription is correct.

– PAGE 86 –
L-SHAPED INHERITANCE

2,400 miles.

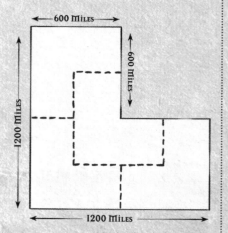

FALCONRY PUZZLE

He doesn't need any extra. The three falcons will catch 100 mice in 100 minutes (they catch one mouse a minute).

– PAGE 87 –
MISSING FISH

Only three people went fishing: a father, his son and his grandson – two fathers and two sons.

CONDEMNED TO DEATH

6 is the best choice: the lions would already have starved to death.